The Garden of Tragedy

Zaeleigh Williams

The Garden of Tragedy
Copyright © 2024 by Zaeleigh Williams.

All rights reserved. No part of this book may be reproduced in any form or by any electronic or mechanical means, including information storage and retrieval systems, without permission in writing from the publisher, except by reviewers, who may quote brief passages in a review.

This publication contains the opinions and ideas of its author. It is intended to provide helpful and informative material on the subjects addressed in the publication. The author and publisher specifically disclaim all responsibility for any liability, loss, or risk, personal or otherwise, which is incurred as a consequence, directly or indirectly, of the use and application of any of the contents of this book.

MILTON & HUGO L.L.C.
4407 Park Ave., Suite 5
Union City, NJ 07087, USA

Website: *www. miltonandhugo.com*
Hotline: *1- 888-778-0033*
Email: *info@miltonandhugo.com*

Ordering Information:
Quantity sales. Special discounts are available on quantity purchases by corporations, associations, and others. For details, contact the publisher at the address above.

Library of Congress Control Number:	2024926095
ISBN-13: 979-8-89285-409-2	[Paperback Edition]
979-8-89285-402-3	[Digital Edition]

Rev. date: 11/20/2024

Chapter 1
Rotten Apples

The apple doesn't fall far from the tree,
Could it be,
that an apple like me can only be rotten,
If left forgotten it might be,
True I am not my forefather,
but my mind was made by no other, have I soured?
It could have been an hour,
To save a savory taste,
but still,
I have gone to waste,
Would I still have been sour had I been born a flower?
What troublesome thoughts,
if I am to rot alone,
But no accompanying me is the fruit of my tree.
Am I blind?
My family to me is kind,
We came from the same tree.
Did they create me?
If I have not fallen far are they also below par?
I know of the rotten few,
but also the perfect fruit,
Only to find this untrue,
as the apple doesn't fall far from the tree,
They all fell the same as me

How my heart dies when thinking of the time,
The daughters and sons of a family shunned,
bitten by the snakes, claimed by insanity,
Punished by humanity,
the citrus fruits born to a tree distantly related to me,
Tough and sour once were flowers,
never savory sweet,
tragic ends met to them by their own feeble feats,
oh, tears will be cried as they have all dried,
fallen from the tree,
never forgotten,
but still so rotten that it makes a monster blink,
He may even cry tears for those lost to the tree's disease.

The most sour,
never a flower,
Was the mindless lime,
not too kind and far too blind,
he brought terror to their tree,
he first defiled the flower,
only half-sour to take a bite of her sweet,
his own twin from a different man,
turned bittersweet,
Her eyes were bright he took that light,
tainting them with lemon and tangerine.
When she called for help from a root of her place,
They turned her away with no dismay,
and told her to stay in her place,
never again would she trust a man derived from her tree.
Soon she'd find the perfect guy an apple rotten but sweet.

The sweetest of the tree,
much more so than the tangerine,
Was the orange queen.
Born from the mindless lime and woman ignorant but kind,
She never had a chance against the man,
who had previously hurt her aunt,
He came to her,
A sapling so unsure,
the time was yet before you could guess,
the horrid lime had in his mind the beautiful orange queen,
He stole again from his kin before she could even blink,
an evil man,
only god could stand,
had turned a darker green
Taking what would make a girl into a woman,
but never would go punished,
Still despite this crime,
she'd never sour like the lime,
even with a little time,
Shed also go to her tree for some reprieve,
again they'd turn away a fruit hurt by his ways,
She asked a mango for a place to go but still found no home.
So she ran from the man far as she could stand,
Only to come back with sweetness still intact,
With her,
a daughter innocent as can be,
a husband she found who was perfectly round,
her and her plum began anew,
but the poor fruits would have yet to see their tragic meet.

The lemon though different from the lime,
always led a pathetic life,
by the time he was only four,
his mind was hell to endure,
Always in trouble lost in a bubble of sin and shame,
the man never had a chance in life's twisted game,
When man has been evil from the beginning,
kindness is lost in editing,
the lemon had always tried to show kindness between his sour lies,
though some could say he was far too blind,
The doctors knew him well,
he was aware that he was ill,
never could he have known that he would betray one of his own,

Sweet as can be the orange queen had a soft spot for his kind,

as he did differ from the lime,

He stayed amongst her orange grove,

Happy in his newfound home,

but one fight is all it takes,

For him to betray his sacred place,

 his dark ways had gone too far,

her favor he had fallen from,

Blinded by a pained rage he committed his worst mistake,

He struck down the orange queen with a shining metallic piece,

her eyes wide as she saw,

he wasn't in there anymore,

he jabbed the blade into her side until her breath slowly died,

It wasn't till her eyes had dulled that he felt his heartstrings give a pull,

He fled the scene eyes full of tears as he had just committed his deepest fears,

she was found by her blossom a little sprout,

dull and lifeless no words would come out,

He did pay for his crimes,

the light never did return to his eyes,

He was found one day as lifeless as can be,

at the bottom of my tree.

The pineapple,
a stand-up type,
Always doing what is right,
Differed from the others of our tree,
Anger was never his thing,
A kind man with a large soul,
He gave his all and much more,
Despite his pacifist ways,
He joined the army to fight for his seeds,
The gardens ideals were still strong in his leaves,
He grew far below our tree,
But to this day still stands higher than me,
Though sadly he is but a memory,
A kind man unshaken by war,
Could only take so much to endure,
The ground ran dry not a drop from the sky,
The soil was bitter and dead,
his funds were gone,
His mind was lost to the struggle,
Saplings cried "Hungry am I",
causing his heart to crumble,
Sad was the pineapple,
at god's hard trials,
Feeling forsaken and crazed,
The pressure too much as the ones he loved,
in his mind withered way,
He took his own life outside the gardens gates,

The one to survive sad but alive,
Lived to be gray and old,
Stories she tell of her family's hell,
where beautiful but sad to behold ,
she was a grapefruit saved from the flu that seemed to infect our tree,
sad as I am at least one limb made past forty three.

Chapter 2

Young ?
Does age take from what I've done,
To have endured hell just to face the sun, isn't enough?
Fine I will except I need time but,
never will it ever feel quite right,
Cause in my mind are monsters ,
Fatal imposters,
And they blind my sight from what is wrong and what is right,
Lurking through the trees as they scream silly things till I'm weak,
Then,
their voices they have changed,
slightly evil in complete disarray,
They say the cruelest things laughing as I cry,
mocking what is me,
never will i ever be heard cause all is in blur inside a locked hearse,
that is never ending on a road forever bending,
Man will tell me that I'm strong only to say I am weak all along,
I am lost without sight,
as my action aren't kind,
I visit estranged places in the depths of my mind,
visions unreal create a hell specialized to me,
oh please oh please have mercy on me "oh but, isn't it fun my darling plum to dance in the garden of eve".

Lions would sit and look at him the creator of all men,
He hurt her light and they just sat and stared at the sin,
God saw their crime and in his eyes nothing could be done as they were blind and did not conceive the concept of men

Mango was her name,
kindness wasn't her game,
A bit of a rotten seed,
She never was blind yet acted as though there was no sight for her to see,
Troublesome lads were never that bad,
but good girls were to behave,
A real old soul with no remorse for situations that could have been saved,
She would pick and choose her favorite fruit,
and leave the others to wither away,
She was wise in a crazed light but still listen did all that came,
Her children all find that in there mind one thing stays the same,
for within each child lies a piece of the mango fruit.

Men would lie to the great merlot grape,
She married young her heart strung on the lies of his leaves,
She knew before he told the truth he was full of deceit,
Enraged by him and all other men she kicked him off the tree,
He found this wrong and struck her down,
blinded by his pride,
he swooped her up to dispose of his terrible crime,
God stuck down this foolish clown in payment for his lies,
Karma comes to all it wants within due time.

The black berry child with the pretty smile,
was young when he asked her to play,
His intentions were strong,
he knew he was wrong but still he wanted her that day,
Unknowing she was young and ignorant,
He stole her innocence,
He took her soul at eleven moons old,
His sister too corrupted the fruit,
then left her with a note,
Inside he said to the kid, "I had fun" and his sister did too.

Suicide plagues her mind,
Hands touched her cruel and unkind,
They took away her sight,
claimed her pretty mind,
And so she comes to me.
He's falling from the tree,
Scorched are his bitter leaves,
And bruised are his brittle knees,
And so he comes to me.
Yet again they've taken him in,
They won't let go,
Want him back home,
And so they come to me.
Life is to unsure,
children feel the war,
Parents left unsure,
And so they come to me.
Their falling apart,
They broke each other's hearts,
And don't know where to start,   and so they come to me
But I can't breathe.

I try to be a friend,
To lend a hand,
I could try distance,
distance I can't stand
I fucking hate my friends,
Cause on me they all depend,
I hate this space because nobody's there for me,
I hate the ground cause it doesn't make a sound,
Why doesn't it make a sound?
I need help,
I need to know that i even have a self,
I feel like an empty shell,
I don't do well,
I don't eat and only sleep,
or I don't sleep and only eat.
Sometimes I wanna die only more than sometimes,
And even as I cry I can't fucking die cause the phone is ringing all the time,
Another problem,
And I can't solve them,
Family drama and I can't be bothered,
Cause if I am they all look sad
And suddenly I'm not me,
I'm craving release,
It's all bitter but never sweet,
And quiet honestly….. I CANT BREATHE!

Sickley are the two,
Cherries are sour fruits,
Often coming in pairs,
Bringing on despair,
Often in the hour when the birth of a flower,
Starts to commence,
They play as friends begging the flower to let them in,
But they aren't sweet,
They came from my tree,
They smart to deceive,
But even fools can see,
The murkiness to their green.
A wise fruit told me the truth behind these fiends,
Murder they did an innocent man too drunk to see his feet,
Could've been her but open request she looked away,
They were good friends till the man was locked away.

Chapter 3

As a little flower,
I wasn't aware apples could be sour,
It wasn't till I grew,
That I knew how sour was in fact true when speaking of the fruit,
He could look so sweet the darling bitter fein,
Married in he was my adopted kin,
Adopt me he did,
As a child he was kind but never in sight,
I knew him as my father,
He was the one to love me despite being my tormentor,
I thought the love I knew was true,
But now I ask what is true about my past home,
The one thing I know,
His sadness wasn't always just for show.

I hated the one from who I come,
My suffering was never her pain,
Jatropha,
poison,
She was poison,
Never did she love,
Never did she trust,
Never will she grow I can only hope,
Nothing that's what I feel,
At the thought of her ill,
I relish in the idea of her precious pills,
Stealing from her all thrill,
I venture thought of her left to rot,
Left in pain,
From karma I'll take my pay,
Together we can wallow,
Cry,
Die,
She means nothing to me,
All she brings is pain and misery,
No longer do I hate,
Just feel fear and pain,
No longer do I love,
Instead I soar above attachments that remain,
All except the scars on my, brain,
The memories that remain.
Do you find me cruel?
a bitter fool?
You are not wrong but know it's not all my fault,

She took me to a place,
She allowed me to bed with the snakes,
She held me with distaste,
To her I was a mistake,
The things she did,
Things done to her own kid,
Make others cry,
I smile,
A smile of fear,
A smile of hate,
A smile of pain hidden in that smile,
A plan,
It's ungodly my friend,
I wish I could change but the nightmares have gotten to me it seems,
I no longer know how to let it go,
I only know memories cause me to go,
Go to a place,
A place of pain,
A place where I'm trapped,
Only me,
her,
And the snakes,
So mother look me in the face and tell me my disgrace

Not you,
It wasn't supposed to be you,
You knew,
But still at your worst came the words,
You looked at me that way,
My darling willow tree,
You said those things,
It hurt so much pain,
I trusted only you,
I never knew,
Why did it have to be you,
Did you want me to feel your pain,
The blame I could take,
But the you turned to the part of me only you could see,
You used it as a weapon,
It brought on your intentions, the bruises will heal,
But the internal scar never will.

Snakes are a part of any garden,
They keep it hardened,
They keep it from being sane,
They cast on the blame,
I wasn't the only one attacked by snakes,
You know there's no one to blame,
Children know not of real pain,
Anyways that's what they say,
They can only be to blame innocence is nothing,
…. But shame.

Those who find us rotten,

Have forgotten……they're the ones to blame,

Where but ponds simple bygones,

No one knows our names,

So laugh all you want,

Your the ones at fault,

YOU CAUSED OUR PAIN!

Can we trust our brothers?
Not ones made buy ours but ones made by others,
Men who claim to be our best friend,
Can we women truly let them in?
I wouldn't know I tried but feelings grow,
Shame to say hatred is in our veins,
A man or women can our love began to break,
Words of care fall on deaf ears,
I'd say it can't be,
But vipers love to ruin,
And bonds are not that strong when blood is not involved.

Chapter 4

"Mama look" the girl said as she shook,
"The gardens dead",
The women laughed and shook her head,
"In winter it won't grow but come the spring season
The garden will overflow".
The winter season ends and just as she said the garden is alive again.

Flowers grow in gardens,
They never get harvest,
The fruits all saw this,
Flowers don't bleed,
The fruits and the trees envy these things,
But flowers don't always grow they die and they get old,
Flowers don't always see different things,
They stay in simple means,
Till the day they die then they are thrown away like the vessel of life.

The lily lived in peace,
But pieces of her mind were deceased,
The buds of flowers came to her for the knowledge of hours.
Little did they know,
And never would she show that once the pieces go,
 Along comes the poison rich with wanting,
Wanting for release.
Along comes a friend a voice within her head,
"Do it" it said,
So lily went home her family loving knows,
She wasn't right,
She took her saplings lives,
Her mate would cry only to soon die,
Lily's venom spread to her hands from her head.
She lived without judgment from the ones who could help
Of course poisonous plants latch on to their flaws and deny so the innocent fall into their claws.

"Come help me",
Would u answer the call even if u knew it would result in the end of it all,
The tree was weak and begged for help,
No one would come,
all weren't dumb,
But the poor vine couldn't help but acknowledge the cry,
So he lended a hand to help the tree stand,
The tree again begged for help from a friend,
The vine so kind,
offered a hand to help the tree stand,
The vine now small felt weaker then all,
But when he heard the cry he knew in his mind,
He'd have to answer the call,
He offered it all to keep the tree tall,
But never again will the vine stand.

Dandelions are not claimed in the garden,
Dandelions have not been hardened,
They grow wild and free,
No restraints on amount or beauty,
But dandelions lose their heads,
There picked from the patch and blown till there dead,
There cut when not wanted,
And used as an object,
So fear not dandelions your welcome in my garden,
I know you have hardened,
Your heads will be safe within my garden gates.

My sunflower,
She grew by the hour,
She was long and strong,
my beloved one,
She was hung,
Strung from above,
Ripped from,
My darling seed,
And our beloved garden,
Witch they said,
Her eyes blue were sad when she died,
My sweet wild one,
She tried to heal the broken and unreal,
Now she's gone and with her the sun,
Sweetly may you rest,
I'll pay for you a bed,
My sunflowers will grow on top of the sunflower I once loved.

Narcissus isn't a narcissist,
His family's name frames him,
He grew up kind but surrounded by thyme,
Theme said don't run from your head,
Narcissus can't stand his head,
It tells him he's dead,
So he should just die,
Thyme always ask why,
But why isn't the question,
It's just the message,
His father makes it his crime,
His mother makes him cry,
He's giving to those who are kind,
But not kind are receivers,
There believers in evil genes,
Making him an evil thing.

Chapter 5

The cherry blossoms don't have flaws,
There perfect,
They smile with pearl white teeth,
Blush pink cheeks,
And always stay graceful,
But are they stable?
Do cherry blossoms feel real,
Not if they never kneel,
And so they never kneel,
Or smoke drugs or take pills,
But how do they feel?
They can't feel,
There unreal,
Blossoms have the urge but never splurge,
Blossoms cant,
There perfect its fact,
But is only a truth,
Passed onto their youth.

Mary have mercy,
The garden is thirsty,
The seasons dry,
One at a time were all soon to die,
Mary please my mother is weak,
I know we have sinned,
both women and men,
But we mean no harm,
Bear no ill will to our brothers in arms,
We know what we do,
Such is the weight of our fruits,
But surely my tribe doesn't deserve to die,
"For children and men are no different,
Focus only on your pain,
Not the pain of the sane,
Your life might be young but decided it's done".
Oh Mary why,
"Because my child you are blind".

"I was never yours",
The words were haunting for sure,
The flooded his mind,
Repeating all the time,
"I was never yours",
He wasn't sure if she meant it,
But he knew she didn't regret it,
He'd left his bumble bee for a lady,
Now his heart was breaking,
The lady left,
and his bumble bee's words were stuck in his head.
How could she have left him for dead?
After all he gave,
All he said,
But he had left,
Even after all bee did,
After all she said,
Karma was a bitch.

Be still basil,
Patience or be ill,
Be kind thyme,
Don't try to conceive,
Don't cry cumin,
You're not human,
Your fine rosemary,
Sadness is temporary,
Be better than this said the mist,
"What about me",
Clover,
you are nothing but a weed.

My heart bleeds,
Soaking into the soil edged beneath,
The rich sea of trees
Wildebeest,
Benevolent things,
My heart bleeds,
In a garden hardened,
My heart bleeds,
If I need to see I will see,
If I need to speak I will speak,
But not everything,
Regardless my heart bleeds,
You and me it's not destiny,
Yet my heart bleeds.

I still don't know what it means to be a weed,
I don't know how to be a flower,
I was never a fruit,
I'm not a tree,
I'm not a bug,
What am I,
I asked a dove,
She scoffed,
I know I'm not a hoe,
I've been called one though,
I'm not pretty,
Not like a daisy,
But I'm not ugly according to the lazy,
I just don't know what it means to be a weed.

I'm conscious of the unconscious,
I'm scared of the safe,
And happy when afraid,
I'm filled with rage,
But on the verge of a mental break,
My mind isn't sane,
But I'm not crazed,
I do not doubt being doubtful,
I do not trust in my own lust,
Nor my own love,
But I trust in trusting nothing.

Chapter 6

Some days I wish I was dead,
Butterflies can lose their heads,
People can say things they wish they hadn't said,
Flowers can envy the free,
Fruits can bleed,
Trees can see,
So why can't I wish to be deceased?

Who am I?
Why do you ask?
Do you want to discover the past,
Can you look at the tainted grass,
See the stained edged into the soil,
Or do you wish to know what I do,
Not what I've been through,
Then do you wish to see,
The scarred from me,
 the darker seems in this bad story,
The night full of fights,
The times filled with cries,
The screams all my own,
Do you want to know?

As young girls fruits are flowers,
To desire a flower is sin,
But seeds don't care from who they grow,
And bugs think loves eternal,
So many young flowers wound up paternal at a young age,
Their age is grave,
But not the sin of the tortured men,
The flowers sin alone,
No matter how a flower feels,
Her child's a bastard when grown,
No matter how the flower works how her child matures,
No matter who the child is,
It's nothing but a sin,
No matter who we wished to be,
fates decided by the trees.

Flowers can be deadly,
Fruits can bleed,
Grass can scream
What could I do?
 and who could I be?
That's all up to you,
come May or June you turn to a dove,
Or fall of the rug,
Then you'll know,
Only a bit at a time till you've grown,
Then you'll start to die right when you've figured out life.

The white lotus was sad,
Although her life wasn't bad,
big things made her feel bland,
And so did the things she'd think,
Things that made her weak,
Her mind wasn't kind it'd call her blind,
She was afraid,
In pain,
And no one could see,
She pondered and wondered,
"How do I stop suffering"?
She could've tried talking,
But her family wasn't kind,
And they say she's lying,
So she kept it in,
The fears the doubts,
They grew into voices and sounds,
Which grew into cuts and drowning,
Then she left early,
One day she didn't wanna stay,
But the want had been for days
When she finally did what couldn't be undone,
From my tree she hung,
Now tainted red,
The white lotus is dead.
She's not insane just in pain,
Who's to blame?
Those who make her feel weak just because she didn't speak,
Those who didn't care to listen to her fears because it caused them tears,

Those who didn't hear her cries because they were to wrapped in their owns lies,
Those who didn't stay,
Those who screamed blame,
The blaming words the last thing she heard,
But is it their fault they had lives of their own?

You try too hard,
You don't try hard enough,
You laugh too hard,
You don't laugh near enough,
You cry too much,
You never cry hard enough,
You beg too much,
You didn't beg near enough,
I care about you,
But not that much.

Kids find kids,
They become friends,
Until they kiss,
What Fun it is,
Then comes "love",
Its accidental lust,
Then comes drugs to increase the fun,
Sex and drugs,
Kids having fun,
Till she takes the test,
He makes the guess,
They say they'll try,
And maybe they might,
But most won't instead they'll give up,
Few will have the sense to give creation to better hands,
Some will do so well,
While others live in hell,
Tell me what's become,
Of all that fun.

Chapter 7

Mad is child,
Blind is the hat upon his head,
The wretched men,
The golden rule of ugly fools,
The wicked hand of a husband,
The cruel stare of an evil hare,
A father's love is just unfair.

The mad hatter is the only man I don't find mad,
The wicked witch was endearing,
The gargoyles comforting,
That's why thyme said I'm blind,
But hades had reason,
And Rasputin was smart,
And Mother Gothel was protective at the start,
Peter pan stole hooks hand,
Usually a villain's pain is for the heroes gain,
So I do believe the red queen will always bleed.

When raven lost her mind,
She had already lost her sight,
Hearing was the first to go,
Her chirps now shrieks could be hard bellow,
Her jubilant personality now full of greed,
It was caused by loss of hatchling,
The garden took on the lonely black dove,
But the loss was simply too much ,
more and more of her started to decay,
Mentally she became a slave,
A slave to pain,
A slave to grief,
See she believed it was her sin,
Her child died from within,
But this was not a sin just a gift hidden,
The hatchling was saved from life's mist,
Saved from the haze,
Or just slain in war,
War of the poor,
Or maybe there's no reason it's just life.

Might I have a bit of pie,
Will I die?
To eat fruit for the few its old news,
But it's forbidden don't eat your brethren.
The smell is sweet juices flowing sweet,
So tempted to try to eat apple pie,
But I cannot or I'll rot,
Or will I?
Just one bite oh but now I want two,
The body's pile,
bloodied fruit,
One more bite,
In my mind it's not a crime,
Please take one more bite.

The whispers,
The intruding thoughts,
They start as murmur,
Then become a deafening roar,
Morality torn,
The flames they dance,
You're put in a trance,
You are the moth you'll never win,
The lighter ignites,
fireflies,
harsh smoke.
  You start to choke,
The feeling warm against your throat,
You're the flame,
The gasoline,
The destruction of things,
Inside your head the flames never dead,
So you burn down the garden,
Leaving only the gates,
They'll say "this was no mistake".

Inside a pear is a seed,
Seeds grow,
New pears form,
But just because you're from a pear doesn't mean you're gonna be green,
You could be yellow or rotten brown,
Just because mothers sane doesn't mean your sound,
Just because fathers grey doesn't mean you'll brown,
It's a simple part of life,
To find out who you are,
Regardless of whose seed you started as.

Flying is like dying,
Death is a myth,
Your carbon marks the sand,
We will know where you've stood,
But you can't sit down,

It's okay to cry,
I promise you everyone wonders why,
Just remember there's been light,
Without it you wouldn't know you've lost sight.

Chapter 8

I feel drained,
The smallest task feel like the biggest pain,
Everyday I see your face,
I love it but hate it all the same,
The work and care,
Have become too hard to bare,
Every ounce stayed with you,
I couldn't stop the hell you didn't mean to put me though,
You take and take but never give,
And the mental strain was evident,
But still you never cared to ask,
Because you needed me as your cast,
I fixed up all your broken bones,
And broke all mine to make a home,
And all that's left of my past self,
Is a garden in the western wing,
Where ravens and black doves sing.

Would you love me if I was a rat,
"Even more then if you were a bat",
Would you beat me if I was a rug,
"Only if there was a bug"
Would you kiss me if I was old,
"The exact same as I did before",
Then I'll love you forevermore.

Before me,
Before her,
Before the drugs,
Before they said you weren't enough,
There was you,
Abusing the person you knew because you didn't see…
You

The moon plants dance,
They dance in circles,
They are special,
I'm not special,
I'm a broken petal,
They dance in circles never feeling unspecial,
But they lose their petals,
The moment the moon settles.

There are men who love,
There are women who don't,
There are children who cry,
And children who die,
But hardly ever is there a person who feels worth it.

Tell me why,
Tell me why thyme,
You watched narcissist cry,
You watched the mist lie,
You watched clover die,
You watched the garden dry,
You watched the apples rot,
And yet,
There you stand,
Blameless,
Nameless,
But neglect is still an offense,
You're not innocent,
But innocence you claim,
Even though you're partly to blame.

Never,
Never again will I trust,
Never again will I love,
Love like I loved,
Never will I feel that pull,
Never again will I spill,
Never again will I feel,
Feel what I felt,
Not because I can't just because I don't want to.

What am I?
A garden full and I'm unsure,
I don't look pure,
My brothers are pears,
I'm not a pear,
I'm to sour,
My sisters are flowers,
I never flowered,
What if I've been devoured
A ghost in the shadows,
Shadows exposed,
I'm exposed,
How far?
How far will this go?
How long?
How long will I show?
Before I fade,
Drift away,
Gone in the wind,
 as if I'd never existed.

Chapter 9

I give you win,
I cannot live,
At Least not like this
I fear the mist,
I fear how it twist,
Whispers that exist,
Only to hurt,
Hurt the dirt,
Till it dies,
When the mist dies,
The gardens gone,
That's the song,
We all secretly sing,
Hoping one day we will be set free.

Some seeds run,
They run far,
They run fast,
Till they find,
Life they find,
Life where existence instinctively causes crime.

Autumn comes taking the leaves of the young,
Then winters freeze kills the trees,
Springs rain brings them back again,
Summers heat kills their glow,
But I still remain through it all.

"Pull the weeds" man screams,
The trees quietly agree,
The fruits smile wickedly,
"but their pretty" the boy says with pity,
The flowers agree blind to see,
The weeds invade breaking unbroken things,
The weed invade destroying remains,
 Remains that remind him,
Remind him of the mist.

Dear tree,
You empathize with me,
But never try to save,
Your children from the pain,
You cry but do nothing,
Always saying something,
But never to,
Those who do what hurts,
Only to those who don't deserve,
Deserve to know who we are and were,
But still you can say,
"They're not okay",
To everyone but the cause,
Where do your calls go,
I never know,
Never to who is needed,
Excuses proceeded,
Conversation gets heated,
I receded,
Fearing getting overheated,
But now I still need it,
Serious commitment.

Love is a blossoming nightshade,
Beautiful and calming,
But you can feel your heart stopping,
Every touch more disrupting,
Till your breath is heavy,
Your brain in a tizzy,
Fights for consciousness,
Then suddenly,
Nightshades dealy giving you no pity,
Taking it stops giving,
Then erupts the panicked feelings,
But it's too late for new beginnings.

Give it a day then you'll be okay,
Or else that's what they say,
But soon the day ends,
And I know I'll lose all my friends,
One day I'll look up,
And will have lost the sun.

Lily of the valley,
Not close to my lowly alleys,
How do you take hearts,
Rip them apart,
And still be called art,
When the heart that's ripped is always mine,
Even though I try,
I'm becoming dry,
Bitter sour,
Those were last hour,
An hour ago I wasn't this old,
But in a minute this will be young,
Lily you stay young,
You don't become plump,
You're not even dumb
How come I am?
Am I wrong for being sad?
I'm just kinda mad,
I never get the man,
Nor the girl,
Just the feels.

Where did all the apples go,
I noticed they disappeared in the snow,
Wondering where they'd go,
Running in the snow,
Trying to find the growth,
Just to find a stump,
I feel my shoulders slump,
Missing what I knew now that I finally grew,
Still unsure of what I am or who I was?
But it sure is fucking lonely growing up,
And I'm not near done.

Chapter 10

People aren't things,
They're beings,
They're simply too wicked to be things,
In control of their entire beings,
They still do wicked things,
Blaming object for their mindset,
But beings are what make an object,
And objects are unloved pets,
Used for different things,
And treated lesser by beings,
Beings like us,
Those unsure of who they was or were,
Different but unsure,
Of what they are,
Watched from afar.

Isn't it funny,
How life becomes so lonely,
A world of people,
And still isolation is legal,
It's becoming lethal,
For the people,
People like me,
Desperate to no longer be lonely,
But then,
Where does it begin,
To be lonely you must first have a friend,
Then loose to the wind,
Drift into sin,
And lose yourself in the end,
So am I lonely?
Or did I lose me?

Roses are like mirrors,
Everyone loves the idea,
But do any really please you,
Do you see yourself in the reflection,
If so who am I to question,
I simply just don't get the message.

Trees,
The holder of seeds,
The homes of the weak,
But snakes reign,
In summer trees brains,
Animals try to remain,
Praying on the gardens pain,
But thanks to the snakes,
The garden remains sane.

Eat it,
Eve said to Adam,
Since women have sinned,
But never men,
Who decided this,
Lilith left because of this,
Adams pride was the original sin,
His ego bringing pain,
Making us go insane,
The original crime,
Allowing a man in a woman's life.

Were we in love?
Or did we love the idea of us?

Ideas are like emotions you barely feel,
But they become so real,
Giving way to appeal,
A glutinous thrill,
Lust filled,
Till it drops wrath then comes,
Mixed with envy,
Killing memories,
Replacing feelings with thoughts,
Till we've all decided to rot.

Dandelion,
Your brains on fire,
Your minds in ruin,
You're so foolish,
How could he care,
If you were never there,
You were blank,
A wiped slate,
Never the same,
He'll never be the same!
Because you made sure he felt the space,
And now he'll make sure I feel the pain.

Chapter 11

B- broken
I- independent
T- troubled
C- crippled
H- harsh
It takes a boy,
to make a broken,
independent,
troubled by crippling depression and harsh bitch.

How long will you cry lime,
Fake tears of cyanide,
You want it,
You take it,
Need it,
And you disgrace it,
You're impossible,
And harsh as falling in pavement,
But the tree,
Still holds your seeds,
You're sour,
Bitter,
And cruel,
But the tree still loves you,
Even though with me,
The tree discarded my seeds.

Paper comes from wood,
It was over the moment this was understood,
Cause wood comes from trees,
So all the men,
And their kin,
Came into the garden,
And stole our trees for their harvest,
With no care,
For the saplings who bear witness to the act,
Learning,
Lessons they shouldn't know,
Growing cold,
As they watch their mother,
Be hurt by others,
And what of their brothers,
They see power,
Learning by the hour,
How to take,
A lesson is made,
Steal and you shall be saved.

My brothers are pears,
Sweet,
Neat,
The perfect treat,
But often forgotten,
They cause no problems,
So there's no need to solve them,
They have bleeding hearts,
Easily torn apart,
Full of love,
They catch the eyes of doves,
But my sweet boys,
They prefer crows,
Old souls,
They are old souls,
Hearts of gold,
I can't wait to watch them grow,
I just wish they'd rely on me more.

Flowers,
The little seeds,
Siblings to me,
Have grown their stems,
Beginning to bloom in the mist,
Breathtaking gifts,
They are like the mist,
Sweet scents,
Completely innocent,
All daisies waiting to grow,
Beautiful lively souls,
Full of the warmth from home,
Resilient to the snow,
But I see the pressures beginning to fall on you,
I want to help you through,
Please take the hand I extend to you,
And know I wish for the best of you,
But expect your flaws,
Because those are your best qualities all in all.

If I leave,
Don't blame yourself blame me,
The parties that haunt my dreams,
Control how I think,
The demons that crowd me,
I'm no longer a girl,
But I'm haunted like one still,
Remember there is no guilty,
I was claimed,
Long ago by the snakes.

I'm insane,
I'll rot your brain,
My mother always says,
You're the problem,
So blame me,
I need the control it brings,
Oh the securities bliss,
As I enter abyss,
 all the pain,
Starts and ends with me.

I love sunflowers,
In the garden they hold power,
Fair and sweet,
Just ask the bees,
She's just so neat,
Unlike me,
I still don't know,
What or who I am,
But the sunflowers seem to understand,
They get me through the bad,
And never judge my past,
The sun on earth,
The warmth in my heart.

I grew but never knew,
You'll never not grow,
You'll never really know,
Just take it slow,
You allowed to fall,
To gain what's lost,
And begin a new,
To find you.

Most gardens loathe the snow,
But we know,
The snow fall,
Is the greatest blessing of all,
Take out the old,
So we can continue to grow.

Chapter 12

I'm so tired,
Tired of feeling on fire,
My skin burns,
Burns with desire,
Take the flame,
Hold it to my face,
Watch it burn away
I itch for a blade,
One swipe and it goes away,
Give me a day,
A day were the pain isn't craved,
Fantasies of the flame,
Burning me away,
Fantasies of the blade piercing my skin.

If I cry I'll die,
The tears will slide,
Revealing what's inside,
Inside my brain,
Memories of pain,
No control over who hurts me,
Relive it again,
Try to swim,
But I drown,
Lost never found,
Screaming without sound,
So the tears won't slip,
Not when I need to fight,
Fight for others to survive.

Death is a funny thing,
It's the strings,
The knots,
That leads you to your time,
But for now,
All I can do is try,
To make the knots fast,
But still remain in the past,
So tomorrow's strings a new beginning,
Till the day it takes me away.

Epilogue

A garden harden by pain,
Lives lost in harvest,
But this isn't just about us,
Your included in the bunch,
Did you feel the garden's pain?
Or is your own reflected in my words?
Are you unsure?
You could be wrong for what you feel,
But if you weren't you'd have no appeal,
You wouldn't be real,
So fall in my land,
Of pain,
Pain without gain,
But gaining isn't always making,
And making is lost,
Maybe you shouldn't fall,
I could be straight,
But influence isn't my thing,
Please don't listen to me,
These words are your dreams,
Or are they nightmares,
It's up to you to decide this.

www.ingramcontent.com/pod-product-compliance
Lightning Source LLC
Chambersburg PA
CBHW032147040426
42449CB00005B/434